REAL BUGS

IN FLIGHT

 **ADVANCE** PUBLISHERS

 **DeAGOSTINI** COLLECT & DISCOVER

LUNA MOTH

Luna moths are one of the largest moths in the world. They have huge pale green wings with long tails and are shaped like an old-fashioned kite.

With a wingspan of up to 5.9 inches (15cm), which is as wide as the length of a pencil, luna moths are huge. The word lunar means "of the moon," and these moths get their name from the moonlike markings on their wings.

FINDING A MATE

Male luna moths have an impressive sense of smell. During the mating season, the females give off a scent to attract the males. Using their antennae, the males can pick up the tiniest traces of this scent from over 3.7 miles (6km) away.

FAT CATERPILLARS

After mating, the females lay clusters of eggs. The caterpillars that hatch from these eggs have huge heads. The caterpillars grow up to 2.7 inches (7cm) long and change color as they get older. They live on leaves and they must eat as much as they can at this stage. Once they become moths, they can't eat—the adult moth has no mouth!

SHARP SPINES

The caterpillars spin tough cases, or cocoons, of silk around themselves. Inside, they slowly change into moths. The moths pierce their way out of the cocoons with the sharp spines of their wings.

SIZING UP

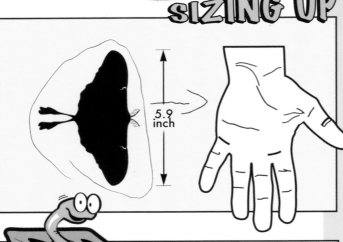

5.9 inch

BEASTLY FACTS

- **SCIENTIFIC NAME:** *Actias luna*
- **SIZE:** 4.7 inch long, including tail; 4.9–5.9 inch wingspan
- **LIVES:** Forests of North America
- **EATS:** The caterpillar eat leaves; the moth doesn't eat anything

TSETSE FLY

Although it belongs in the same family as the housefly, a bite from the tsetse fly could kill you!

The tsetse (say TSET-see) fly lives in tropical parts of Africa, where it feeds on the blood of cattle and people.

DEADLY DISEASE

When a tsetse fly bites, it injects some of its saliva into its victim's skin. This saliva may contain the germs of diseases that can kill cattle and horses, and the germs that could lead to sleeping sickness, which can kill people. A person with sleeping sickness feels extremely sleepy and may eventually die.

A GOOD MEAL

The tsetse fly likes to have a good, long meal and may take up to 10 minutes to suck up all the blood it wants. When it is full, its abdomen swells and turns red (below). It won't need to feed again for about another three days.

SMALL FAMILIES

Unlike other insects that lay eggs, the female tsetse fly gives birth to live young. In her short lifetime of about six months, she may produce only two offspring a month.

SIZING UP

0.79 inch

- **SCIENTIFIC NAME:** *Glossina palpalis*
- **SIZE:** 0.79 inch long
- **LIVES:** Tropical Africa
- **EATS:** Animal blood, including that of humans

BEASTLY FACTS

Imagine walking through a desert under the blazing sun, when suddenly the sky goes black. A cloud has blocked out the sunlight—a cloud of desert locusts.

SWARM!

In a matter of hours, a locust swarm can munch its way through tons of vegetation. No wonder some farmers (above left) take to the air to protect their crops from the locusts.

Desert locusts gather in huge numbers and eat all the crops in their path. They can travel for hundreds of miles, and they are particularly common in Africa and Asia.

WEATHER CHECK

For desert locusts to go on a rampage, the weather has to be just right. Usually only a few of the eggs that are laid by the females survive. But if weather conditions are good, more eggs hatch. As they become overcrowded and food runs out, the young locusts swarm. Here are the six stages that result in a swarm.

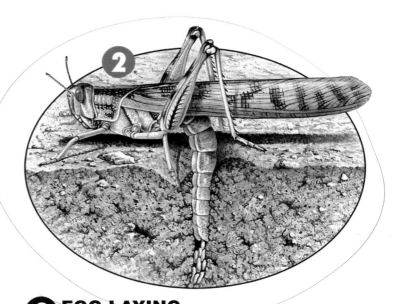

❷ EGG LAYING

After mating, the female lays a pod (group) of sausage-shaped eggs in a warm sandy area. There can be up to 100 eggs in one egg pod. She digs a hole by extending her abdomen and puts her eggs in it. She then blocks the hole with some froth, which she makes in her abdomen. The froth hardens to protect the eggs and help prevent them from drying out.

❶ SHOWER POWER

The best time for the females to lay their eggs is after rain. This is because the rain makes the crops grow so there is plenty for the young to eat. Also, it is easier for the babies to get out of the ground when the soil is wet.

❸ HATCHING HOPPERS

The baby locusts hatch after 9 to 11 days. The young locusts are known as hoppers, or nymphs. They are exact miniatures of the adults, only without wings. The young hoppers start to feed as soon as they hatch. They have very strong jaws—perfect for biting into plants.

Small Talk

- As much as 7 million dollars worth of food is lost to locusts each year.
- Locusts are a good source of protein. In some parts of Africa, people eat them.

SWARM!

4

This locust (right) is an adult. It has shed its skin and grown wings. Now it's ready to swarm! Locusts have two phases in their lives: a solitary one, when they live alone; and a sociable one, when they swarm.

4 EATING ON THE MOVE

The hoppers go on a march that lasts four to five weeks. This is when they cause the most damage. There can be 15,000 hoppers per square yard. During the day, the young locusts hop in groups called bands. At dusk, they feed. Their favorite foods are corn, millet, citrus fruits, and wild grasses.

5 The skin splits down a hopper's back, and the adult begins to emerge.

The new adult turns around and holds

Blood begins to pump around the wings. The adult eats its old skin.

5 TAKING TO THE SKIES

The locust adult (left) grows to full size by molting (shedding its skin). It does this six times in its life. When its four wings are fully grown, it is an adult. It is then able to fly off and find new areas to feed. It flies at 6.2–15.5 miles per hour (10–25km/h), depending on the direction and speed of the wind. During this adult stage, it eats its own weight in food each day.

Small Talk

POOL POISON

Chemicals called insecticides are sprayed to kill pests. It would take nearly 1 million gallons (4 million litres) of insecticide to get rid of a large locust swarm. That's enough to fill four Olympic-sized swimming pools.

6

6 SWARMING

Once the locusts have eaten all they can in one area, they fly off. A typical swarm (above) can contain 10 billion locusts and cover an area of 1,165 square miles (1,875 sq km). A swarm of locusts can eat over 20,000 tons of food each day. Swarms can cause complete devastation to a farmer's field.

BLOWFLY

The blowfly focuses on its next tasty meal. On the menu today are a rotting dead bird, bits of leftover food, and a pile of dung. The blowfly can't chew or swallow solid food. Instead, it vomits some of its previous meal onto the food, which turns it to liquid. Yum! This mixture of rotting food and vomit is sucked up through a special strawlike feeding tube called a proboscis. Perhaps you'll think twice before you invite a blowfly for tea.

HORNET

Hornets are able to attack even large insects such as wasps and bees. A hornet's sting can also be dangerous to humans.

The hornet is one of the largest members of the wasp family. It is also known as the yellow jacket because of its bright coloring. Its vivid orangey yellow and black stripes warn us and other animals to keep away.

NEST BUILDING

Hornets build large papery nests made from wood that they chew to a paste. They make their nests in hollow trees, in the ground, or in an empty building. The nest hangs upside down and is made up of layers of small chambers called cells.

SIZING UP

0.74–1.4 inch

BEASTLY FACTS

- **SCIENTIFIC NAME:** *Vespa crabro*
- **SIZE:** 0.74–1.4 inch long
- **LIVES:** All over Europe, Asia, North Africa, and North America
- **EATS:** Insects and sweet foods

HORNET HOUSEWORK

The queen hornet starts the nest in spring. She lays her eggs inside a few of the cells. Young workers grow from the eggs. When they are a little older, they add new layers of cells, clean the nest, and feed the larvae (young hornets). In the autumn, the old queen and the other hornets all die. Only new queens survive the winter, after which they each start making a new nest.

ELEPHANT HAWK MOTH

In its caterpillar stage, the elephant hawk moth makes itself look more dangerous than it really is.

As soon as the sun sets, the elephant hawk moth begins to fly about, darting from flower to flower to suck up the nectar. It goes on eating late into the night.

UNDER THE LEAVES
The moth lays her eggs on a plant called willow herb. She places the eggs one at a time on the underside of the leaves. Caterpillars hatch from the eggs and later turn into moths themselves.

WARNING SIGNS
The elephant hawk moth caterpillar has a wonderful way of keeping predators away—it fools them into thinking it's a snake! On each side of its head are two large dark spots. When the caterpillar is threatened, it rears up and squeezes its head into its body, changing the shape of the spots and making itself look like a snake's head. Predators get a nasty shock when the dark spots on the sides of the caterpillar's head stand out and look like black eyes.

BEASTLY FACTS

- **SCIENTIFIC NAME:** *Deilephila elpenor*
- **SIZE:** 2.3–2.5 inch
- **LIVES:** Most parts of Europe, North Africa, and Asia
- **EATS:** Nectar from different flowers

SIZING UP

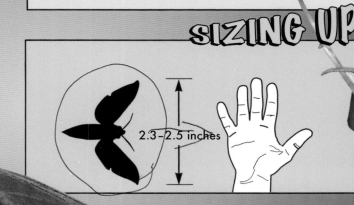

2.3–2.5 inches

ICHNEUMON WASP

A tiny female ichneumon (say ick-NEW-men) wasp is searching for a moth caterpillar. As it flies through the tall grass, it picks up the caterpillar's scent with its sensitive antennae. Seconds later, the wasp lands next to its victim. The female quickly lays an egg on the skin of the caterpillar, and then flies off to look for more caterpillars to house its eggs. A wasp grub will hatch from each egg. The grub will burrow under the caterpillar's skin and feed on its flesh while the caterpillar is still alive.

SPOT THE DIFFERENCE:

It's summertime. There's a buzzing sound and out of the corner of your eye you spot a stripy insect. Is it a bee, or is it a wasp?

Wasps and bees both belong to the same group—Hymenoptera (say hi-meh-NAHP-teh-rah)—which means "filmy wings." But if you take a close look, you'll find that bees and wasps are really different.

Barbed sting. A bee can only sting once.

Two pairs of wings

Golden body

Fluffy thorax and abdomen

"Baskets" for collecting pollen

Proboscis for sucking nectar

BEE

Mixing pollen and cleaning

Dark face—no warning colors

A CLOSER LOOK

Honeybees and common wasps may seem similar—they both have two pairs of wings, small waists, and three pairs of jointed legs—but look closer. Their coats are different colors. Wasps are yellow and black (that's why they are also called yellow jackets), but bees are more orange with thin bands of black. Bees are also a bit fluffier than wasps.

RIGHT BETWEEN THE EYES

If you want to tell if a bug is a wasp or a bee, look it straight in the eye! Wasps have a yellow face with black marks on it, while bees' faces are almost all black with tufts of orange hair.

BEES AND WASPS

WASP

Yellow markings on the face

Thin waist

Smooth abdomen

Stings as often as it likes

Jaws

Yellow markings on the face

Powerful jaws for chewing prey and wood

Yellow and black warning colors

Is it true...

that bees and wasps have two pairs of wings?

Yes. Although bees and wasps look like they have just one pair of wings, they all have two pairs. The rear ones are slightly smaller and are attached to the front ones by several tiny hooks known as hamuli (say HAM-yeh-lie).

Close-up of the hooks that join a bee's front and back wings together

Hamuli

PARTY PACKS AND LONERS

There are thousands of species of both bees and wasps. Some prefer to live in groups housed in big nests with one queen. These bees and wasps are called social. Others prefer to live alone—they are known as solitary. Honeybees and bumblebees, and common wasps and hornets are some of the most familiar species. They are all social insects.

SPOT THE DIFFERENCE: BEES AND WASP

GIRLS RULE, OK?

Female bees and wasps are the ones that build and repair the nests, and provide food for their large families. In honeybee nests, if the old queen dies, a new one will take her place. Sometimes, the old queen leads a swarm of bees to find a new nest site. Wasps rarely swarm.

On their way to a new nest site, a swarm of bees rests on a fence. Wasps don't swarm.

Young worker bees (left) emerge from hexagonal wax cells inside the hive.

A queen wasp starts building her papery nest.

HOUSES

Both social bees and wasps build nests made up of hexagonal (six-sided) cells. Bees make these cells out of wax, which they produce in glands in their abdomens. Common wasps and hornets make their nests out of "paper" by chewing wood into a pulp and spitting it out again.

BAD LADIES

Bees have special brushes and pollen baskets on their back legs that they use to pick up and carry pollen. Wasps don't collect pollen for their young, so they don't have carrier bags or brushes!

QUEEN WASPS GET STUCK IN

In the spring, it is up to the queen wasp to build the nest. She lays the eggs and looks after the young until workers are born to help her. Unlike wasps (and bumblebees) queen honeybees can never set up a home alone because they can't produce the wax to build the cells of the nests. They need help from worker bees before they move in and start laying eggs.

WHAT THEY EAT

Wasps eat meat and nectar, while bees are strict vegetarians. Wasps feed their young other bugs. They bring the bugs back to their nest and chew them up so they can be swallowed easily. Some wasps prey on bees. Hornets often hang around outside beehives waiting for workers to come home. They grab the worker bees and take them home for their young to eat. Common wasps also attack bees while they are collecting pollen and nectar from flowers. Bees feed their young on pollen and never hunt wasps.

Bees use their long tongues to suck nectar from flowers. It is made into honey back at the nest.

HERE ARE SOME GENERAL RULES ABOUT SOCIAL BEES AND WASPS:

BEE
- Makes honey
- Herbivore
- Pollinates many flowers
- In fall, feeds on stores of nectar
- Stings only once, usually if angered
- On the whole peaceful but will attack if a member of its colony is killed
- Doesn't kill pests
- Has sucking mouthparts
- Swarms
- Makes its nest from wax

WASP
- Doesn't make honey
- Eats meat and sucks sap
- Pollinates few flowers
- Doesn't store pollen or nectar
- Stings as often as it needs to
- Vicious to other insects—kills to feed larvae
- Can kill problem pests
- Jaws
- Never swarms
- Makes nest from pulped wood or mud

SPIKY TAIL

A wasp can sting many times, but a bee can sting only once. A bee's stinger is barbed, which means that it has spikes that point backward (toward its body). Once it is stuck into a victim, the stinger gets lodged in the skin and is torn from the bee. Queen bees have smooth stingers that they can use as often as they like. When a new queen bee hatches out of her egg, she has to kill the other queen bee larvae. This is why she needs a reusable stinger.

When a bee stings, it gives off a smell. Other bees fly in and help attack the predator.

PEST PATROL

Wasps do have some good qualities. They can help keep the number of crop pests down. They need to catch a lot of insects to feed their growing young. Several thousand insects are needed to support just one wasp nest!

HOME ALONE

Some solitary wasps are parasites. These wasps lay their eggs inside large bugs, which act like hosts. The host provides the newly born larva with a meal when it hatches. Bees never eat other bugs or their larvae.

FLIGHT OF THE BEE

Take a careful look at wasps and bees as they fly about. Wasps dart around, while bees have a lazier style of flying.

Solitary wasps are attracted to the rotting body of a wild pig in the Amazon jungle.

MICRO MOTH

Dusk is falling and the rain clouds are gathering. With its long, sensitive antennae swept back, a tiny female micro moth takes to the air. Although she has only a 0.19 inch (5mm) wingspan, this moth is an excellent flyer. She can easily dodge the large raindrops as she flies around. The micro moth is looking for a sheltered hawthorn bush and will lay her eggs on its leaves.